ABOVE CARMEL, MONTEREY AND BIG SUR

(*Opposite*) South toward Big Sur

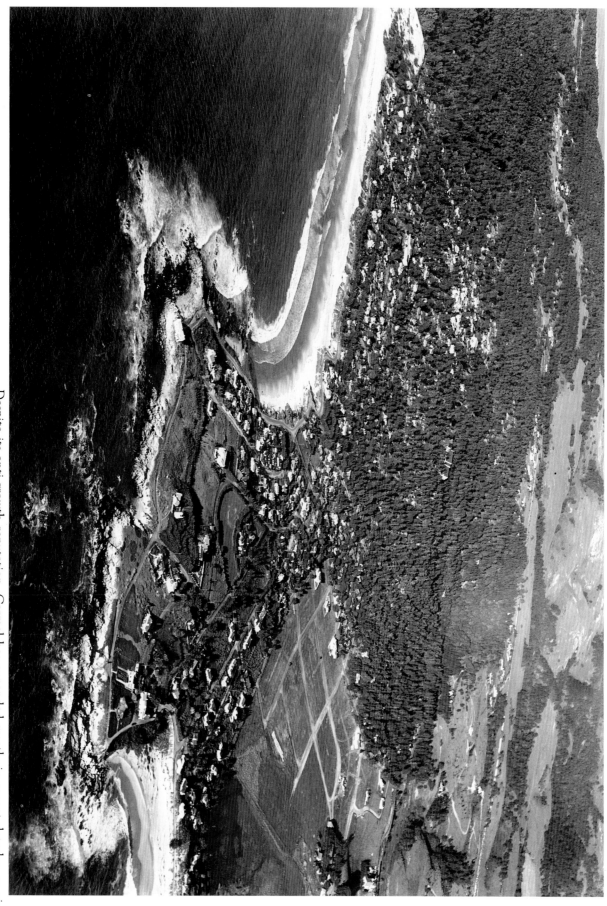

Despite its anti-growth reputation, Carmel has expanded greatly in recent decades, as vividly illustrated in these pictures of Carmel Point in 1938 and 1993. In the contemporary picture, the green-roofed house designed by Frank Lloyd Wright is visible at the left end of the point. To the right is the mouth of the Carmel River.

This is the place where California began.

It began here geologically when the Coast Ranges rose out of the Pacific to form the western edge of North America.

It began here historically when the Spaniards chose Monterey Bay as the site for the capital of California, the westernmost outpost of the Spanish empire.

Visit this coast now and you can have a direct experience with both of these beginnings. See it from the air, as you will in Robert Cameron's pictures, and you will enjoy it with the broadest perspective of time and space.

You can see State Highway 1 clinging to the clifftops down the Big Sur shoreline, traversing the precipitous slopes of the Santa Lucia Mountains, which seem to have just risen from the sea, the water still streaming down the western flanks in creeks and rivers, the white breakers exploding on the cliffs below.

The range is in fact still rising. The road in some places is laid on broad shelves planed off by the ocean when the range was lower and in other places cuts across the rising cliffs that are being continually reshaped by the waves coming in from the far Pacific.

You can imagine the amazement of Juan Rodríguez Cabrillo, the first European explorer to see this coast, when in 1542, sailing for Spain, he fought his way northward through storms that battered his two vessels. Through rifts in the low clouds he caught glimpses of this rising edge of the continent: "So great was the swell of the ocean that it was terrifying to see, and the coast was bold . . . mountains which seem to reach the heavens, and the sea beats on them. Sailing close to land, it appears as though they would fall on the ships."

After such threatening terrain, Cabrillo was doubtless relieved to find shelter in Monterey Bay, which he called "Bahía de los Pinos" for the forests of pines on the coastal hills. The course of New World exploration was painfully slow, and it was more than two centuries before the emissaries of the Spanish empire were able to plant a colony on this shore and create California as a political entity.

This historic beginning, too, you can experience here — in Carmel's Mission San Carlos Borromeo, founded by Father Junípero Serra in 1770, and in the Presidio of Monterey, established at the same time by Gaspar de Portolá. Although Serra first erected a cross designating the site for the mission in Monterey, he soon decided to locate it over the hills by the Carmel River, for reasons you can see in Cameron's pictures. The fertile bottom lands of the river held greater promise for agriculture, and the stream itself afforded an ample supply of water. Serra may also have been motivated by a desire to put a suitable distance between his native neophytes, particularly the women, and the military garrison at the Presidio.

The good padre, who is buried in Carmel at his headquarters mission, has been nominated for sainthood for his incredible feat of organizing the chain of California missions, which converted to Christianity thousands of the native residents. But the nomination has caused dissent among those who find his work misguided. He attracted the Ohlones and members of other tribes into the mission, baptized them, and taught them weaving and farming. In the process, however, the native culture was wiped out, hundreds died of European diseases, and the survivors were unable to resume the ways of their ancestors when the missions crumbled into disuse a few decades after they were established.

However, the mission regime of the padres was benevolent compared to the later impact of the Yankees, who slaughtered the natives without compunction. The only present-day reminders of the original Ohlone society are the shell mounds along the coast and in the river valleys — the sole remnants of their villages and encampments, vestiges of a vanished culture.

Fortunately, there are ample remains of Monterey's era as the provincial capital. At the edge of the harbor, near the foot of the Presidio where Portolá and Serra landed in 1770, you can see the Old Custom House built by the Spanish in 1814, the first public building on the Pacific Coast. It was here that Commodore Sloat raised the Stars and Stripes on July 7, 1846, bringing California into the Union. Nearby are several other buildings dating from Monterey's era as the state capital, including Colton Hall, where the California Constitutional Convention was held.

It is fitting that many of Cameron's pictures in this book were taken from above the ocean and show the relation between land and sea. The ocean dominated this region in many ways. One of them was noted by Robert Louis Stevenson when he lived here briefly in 1879:

The one common note of all this country is the haunting presence of the ocean. A great faint sound of breakers follows you high up into the inland canyons; the roar of waters dwells in the clean, empty rooms of Monterey as in a shell upon the chimney. The woods and the Pacific rule between them the climate of this seaboard region. On the streets of Monterey, when the air does not smell salt from the one, it will be blowing perfumed from the resinous tree-tops of the other.

After the Gold Rush, California's capital was moved from Monterey to Sacramento, closer to the scene of the action, but the removal of the capital did not turn the city into a ghost town. The Monterey Peninsula's potential as a tourist attraction was detected early by the "Big Four" builders of the Central Pacific Railroad (later Southern Pacific),

Robinson Jeffers' Tor House and his stone tower face the ocean at center, set back from Scenic Road. On the cliff to the right is the "butterfly" house, so-called for its flaring-winged roof. In 1960 the house was flooded by storm waves exploding on the cliff.

(*Opposite*) The old and new buildings of Carmel Mission (center), with the church dating from 1797 at the lower left of the quadrangle. Clint Eastwood's Mission Ranch, with its restaurant, guest houses, tennis courts, and parking lots, is at the lower left, alongside a bend of the Carmel River.

The Highway 1 freeway curves over Carmel Hill, where early in the century stagecoaches once brought visitors from Monterey. The off ramps connect with Highway 68, which leads to Pacific Grove, passing the Community Hospital of the Monterey Peninsula.

THE PENINSULA

The northernmost reach of the Monterey Peninsula is the headland that explorer Sebastian Vizcaíno in 1602 named Punta de Pinos — Point of Pines — which is now part of Pacific Grove. Beyond Pacific Grove, in the center of the picture, is Monterey, and around the curve of Monterey Bay at the upper left is the community of Seaside. On the peninsula's ocean front the white surf attacks the edge of the land, slowly eroding it. At the far right is Spanish Bay.

20

Here are 1924 and 1993 views of historic Del Monte Lodge at Pebble Beach, now simply "The Lodge." It was built in 1919 as an attraction on the Seventeen-Mile Drive. The original building, in the center of the 1924 picture, is still standing at the left end of the row of white buildings, overlooking the 18th hole of the Pebble Beach golf course. The house at the lower left in both pictures is Canary Cottage, a Prohibition-era gambling hideaway, now a private home. Grazing elk were once a nuisance on the course, and deer are frequently still seen there. The beach pictured here gave its name to the entire community.

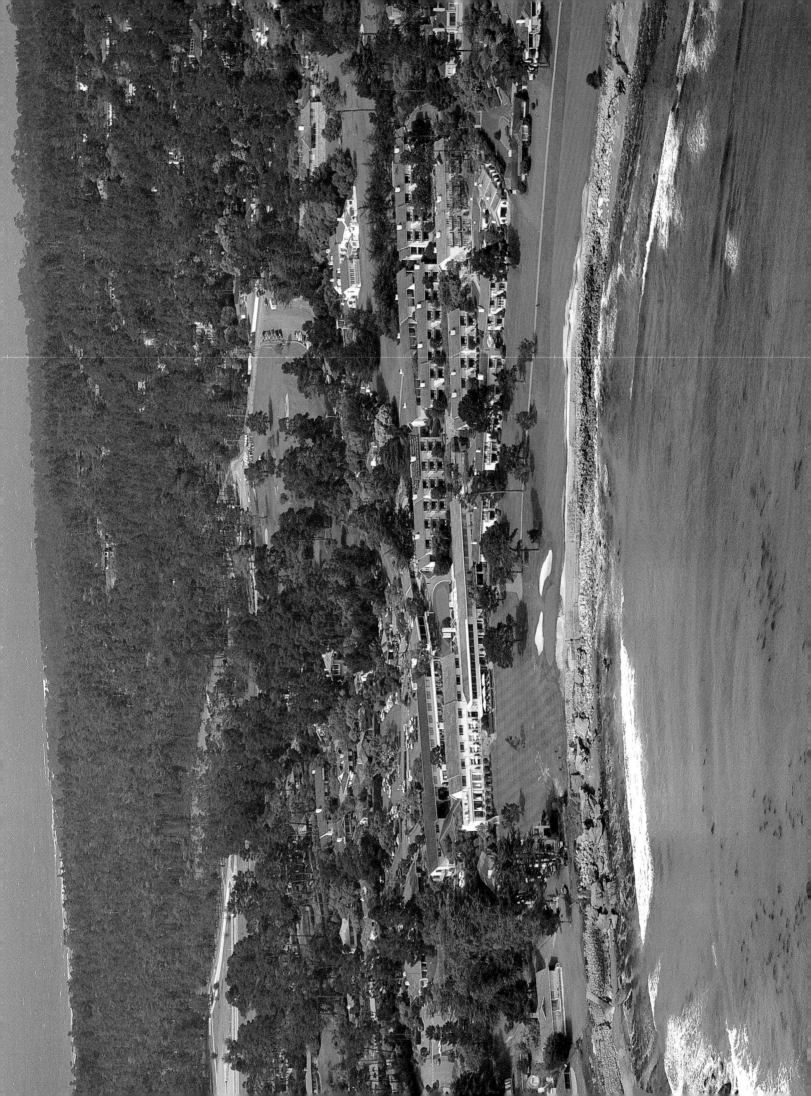

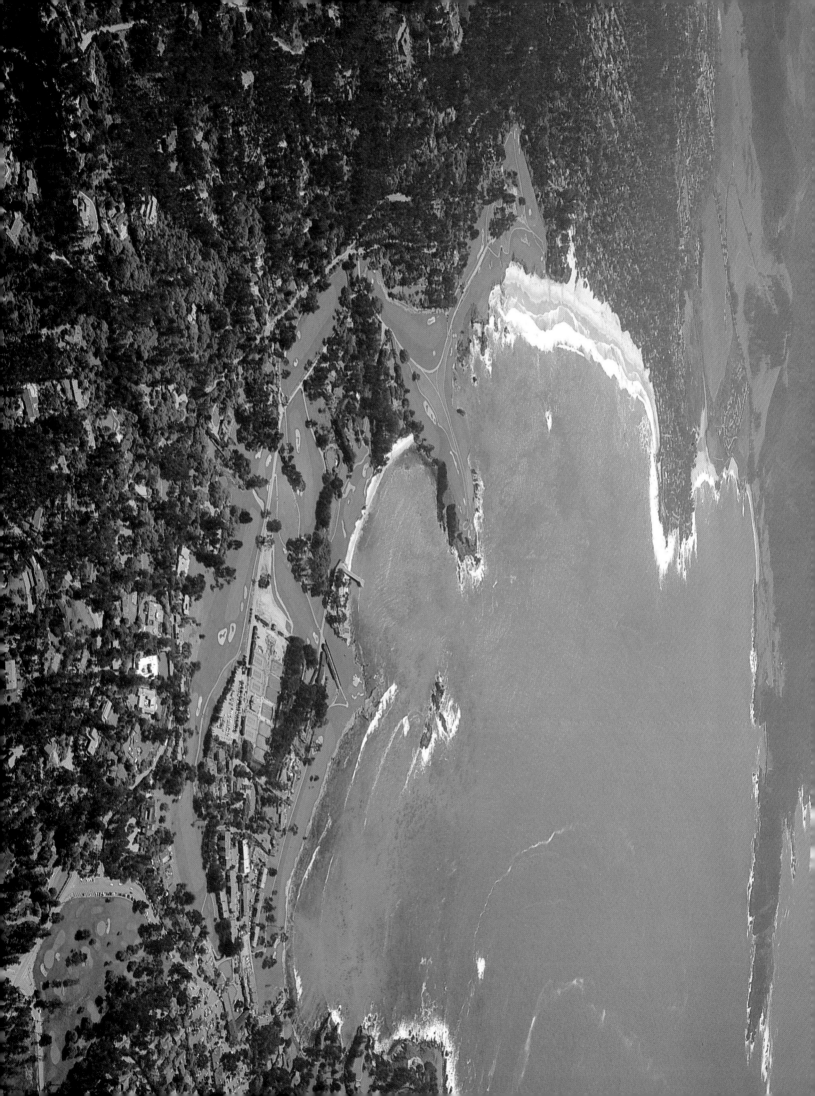

The Beach and Tennis Club, between the Pebble Beach golf course and Stillwater Cove, has been the scene of *haute monde* social events, including "clambakes" hosted by Bing Crosby during the Crosby tournaments of the past. Here in Stillwater Cove Jacques and Philippe Cousteau filmed sea otters in action for a television documentary on the engaging animals.

Adjoining the Pebble Beach course and the buildings of the Lodge on the landward side is the nine-hole Peter Hay course (center), opened to the public in 1957. It was designed by a group headed by Peter Hay himself, a venerable pro from Scotland.

(*Opposite*) The Monterey Peninsula and environs are a golfer's paradise, with a total of 15 courses, several of world class, including this one, the most famous, known in the vocabulary of an earlier era as the Pebble Beach Golf Links. It was designed by championship golfer Jack Neville and opened in 1919. Major tournaments have been staged here since 1929, including the Crosby, now known as the AT&T National Pro-Am, which takes place in January and February of each year, rain or shine (frequently both).

24

North along the shoreline from the Pebble Beach course is the Cypress Point Club, designed by Alister MacKenzie of Scotland and opened in 1928. One of the three greatest holes in golfdom, along with the 7th at Pebble, is the Cypress 16th, pictured here in the foreground. The green is reached from a tee across the water to the left. Over the years a half-dozen golfers have lofted the ball 200 yards for a hole-in-one. At the upper center is Fanshell Beach.

(Opposite) North of Cypress Point is Spyglass Hill Golf Course, designed by Robert Trent Jones Sr. and opened in 1966. The names of the course and the holes, such as "Treasure Island," "Captain Flint" and "Long John Silver," are from Robert Louis Stevenson's novel. This is reputed to be the toughest course on the peninsula. To the left of the course is the Robert Louis Stevenson School.

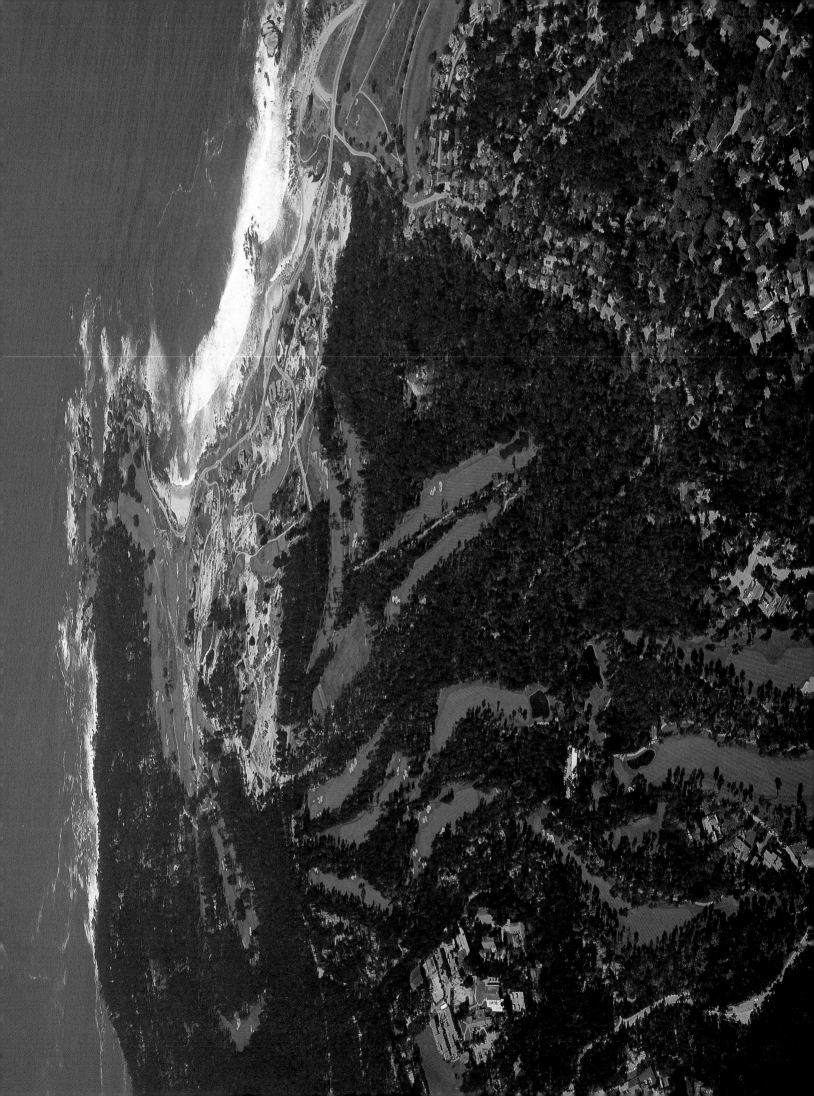

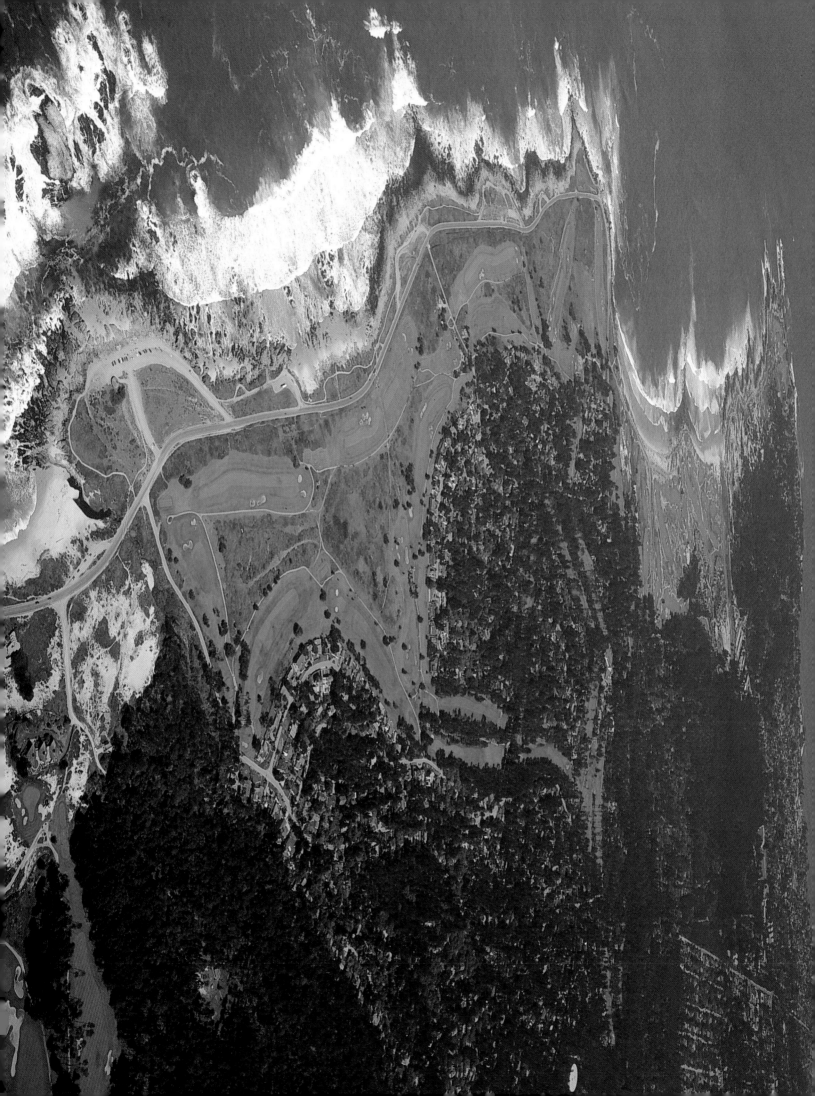

(*Opposite*) North of Spyglass is the private Monterey Peninsula Country Club with two courses, the Dunes Course, laid out by Charles MacDonald and Seth Raynor in 1926, and the Shore Course, designed by R.E. Baldock in 1961. The two promontories at the middle and upper left are Point Joe, named for a Chinese fisherman who lived there, and Point Pinos, named by Vizcaíno in 1603 for the abundant Monterey pines. The Point Pinos Lighthouse, dating from 1853, is the oldest lighthouse on the Pacific Coast. Between the two points is Spanish Bay, possibly named for an encampment of explorer Gaspar de Portolá here in 1769.

The newest of the peninsula's courses is the Links at Spanish Bay. It was designed by Robert Trent Jones Jr., Tom Watson, and Frank Tatum and opened in 1987. It is on the site of a Sahara-like dune field of white Carmel sand, which had been quarried away over several decades.

On the eastern edge of Monterey beyond Highway 1 is the Old Del Monte Golf Course — very old, as golf courses go, dating from 1897 and designed by Charles Maud for guests of the Hotel Del Monte. It began as a nine-hole course and was expanded by nine more holes in 1920 by W. Herbert Fowler. It is the oldest course west of the Mississippi and the first in the world whose fairways were green winter and summer. It has been the site of the California State Amateur Tournament since 1912.

In the pinewood uplands behind Pebble Beach is the Northern California Golf Association's Poppy Hills Golf Course, which opened in 1986, Robert Trent Jones Jr., architect.

(Opposite) Several generations of students and adults have broadened their horizons at meetings here amid the pines and dunes of Asilomar, the conference ground started by the YWCA in 1913, taken over by the State of California in 1956, and later greatly expanded. By the 1990s it was hosting some 50,000 conferees annually. Its eleven original redwood buildings (1913-1928) have been declared a National Historic Landmark. They were designed by architect Julia Morgan. "Asilomar" is very roughly translated from Spanish as "retreat or refuge by the sea."

Offshore from the golf course at Pebble Beach are undersea forests of kelp, growing up from root "holdfasts" on sea-floor rocks. These submarine forests are abundant with marine life, including many species of fish and mammals such as seals, sea lions and sea otters. Storm waves occasionally deposit fish on the golf course.

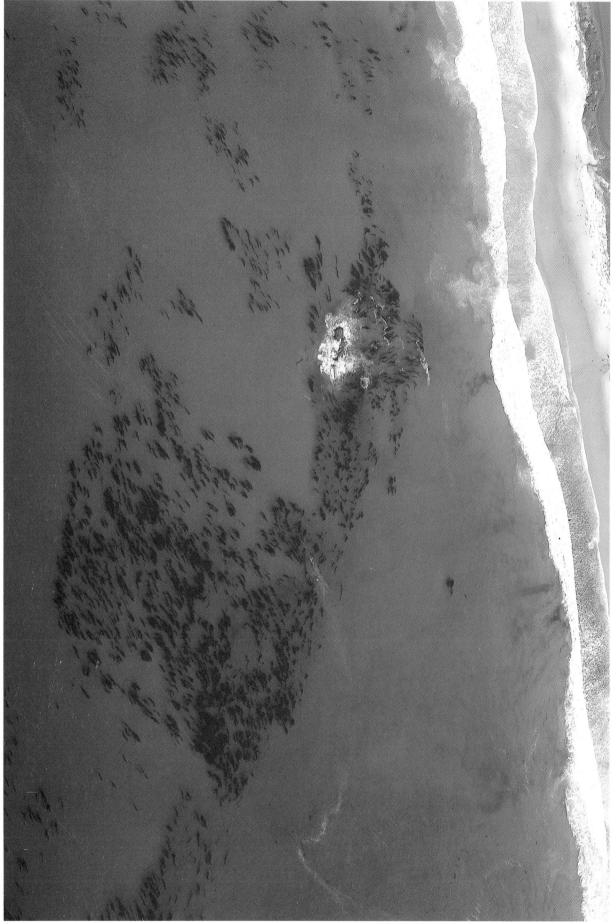

CARMEL VALLEY

The green artichoke fields at the mouth of the Carmel Valley have been farmed for generations by the Odello family. The area on the near side of Highway 1 was preserved as open space by the heroic efforts of Carmel residents, led by former State Senator Fred Farr. It is now owned by the state and leased back for agriculture.

Artichokes thrive only under the kind of climatic conditions found along this coast: sea breezes and intermittent fogs providing cool summers. The subdivision at the lower right is Carmel Meadows. Beyond Highway 1 on the left are shopping centers (see next page), farm plots, and Rancho Canada golf course.

31

As Carmel (upper center) placed strict limits on commercial development within its mile-square boundaries, the open land at the mouth of the Carmel Valley burgeoned with shopping centers and office buildings. At left center are the brown roofs of the Barnyard, including shops and restaurants, where farm-like buildings stand on man-made hillocks amid luxuriant flower gardens. At the right center is the mouth of Hatton Canyon, where proposals for a freeway have stirred a tempest of controversy.

In the foreground is Quail Lodge, rated one of the top resort hostelries in the nation, with its many-laked golf course opened in 1964, Robert Muir Graves, architect. The course and its associated residential areas are hospitable to wildlife, including bobcats, coyotes, deer, raccoons, and wild geese, which are attracted to water holes provided for them. Looking down the valley toward the ocean, we see Hacienda Carmel, a retirement community; Rancho Cañada Golf Club; and Carmel in the far distance.

(Opposite) Looking up the valley, we see farm fields, the Carmel Middle School on the left, and a closer view of Rancho Cañada Golf Club, consisting of two 18-hole courses opened in 1970, Robert Dean Putnam, architect.

Eastward toward the head of the valley are pastures and grassy hillsides that are green in the spring, tawny in the summer. The Carmel Valley Road parallels the meandering course of the river. On the left is the Laureles Grade, leading over the ridge to Highway 68, the Monterey-Salinas Road. To the right of the river is Garland Ranch Regional Park, 3100 acres with picnic grounds and miles of trails. Toward the head of the valley to the left is the airstrip at Carmel Valley Village.

(*Opposite*) A few miles farther up the valley (looking here toward the ocean) is the third of the valley's major golf courses. It belongs to the Carmel Valley Ranch Resort and was opened in 1981, Peter Dye, architect. The resort's guest facilities were opened in 1987.

John Gardner's Tennis Ranch in Carmel Valley, about a mile from the village, attracts socialites and tennis buffs from around the world with its 14 courts in a 20-acre sylvan setting of giant oaks, lawns, and gardens. Gardner, a former tennis pro at Pebble Beach, opened the ranch as a school summer camp in 1957 and developed it into an adult resort a few years later.

Near Carmel Valley Village is the Holman Ranch, a center for equestrian events. The ranch buildings and grounds at the lower left are often used for group picnics, barbecues, and weddings and have sometimes been used as a setting for movies.

(Opposite) The "original" Carmel is 12 miles up Carmel Valley from the ocean. The community here now known as Carmel Valley Village preceded the present town of Carmel in the use of the name. The Carmel Post Office opened here in 1893, serving the valley's ranchers. Ten years later, when the present Carmel applied for a post office, it was named Carmel-by-the-Sea to distinguish it from Carmel in the valley.

Above Carmel Valley Village the valley narrows into a canyon, but there is still room for new vineyards and residential subdivisions along the river. This is the east village area, and the subdivision to the right of the river is named "Camp Steffani," for Joseph Steffani, an early settler.

(Opposite) The Carmel River is the water supply for Carmel and nearby areas. To conserve water and smooth out the seasonal flow, two dams have been built on the river south of the Carmel Valley. This one is San Clemente Dam, first built in 1883 and rebuilt and enlarged in 1921. Part of the upper Carmel Valley is visible at the upper left.

Upstream on the Carmel River six miles above San Clemente Dam is Los Padres Dam, built in 1948. Growing population and increasing water use have resulted in proposals to build a much larger dam, flooding the existing structure. At the upper right is the Cachagua Valley, tributary to the Carmel Valley and the site of abundant new vineyards, where the fog-free climate and summer warmth have helped produce distinctive wines.

(Opposite) In the Jacks Peak area, north of the Carmel Valley, rolling meadows, green in winter, alternate with oak woodlands (foreground) and forests of Monterey pines (in the distance). The pines, like redwoods, grow only in the coastal fog belt and are not found farther inland. This is about as far inland as the fog penetrates. The oaks (principally California live oaks) thrive in the drier inland climate. Point Lobos, enclosing Carmel Bay, is visible on the horizon.

42

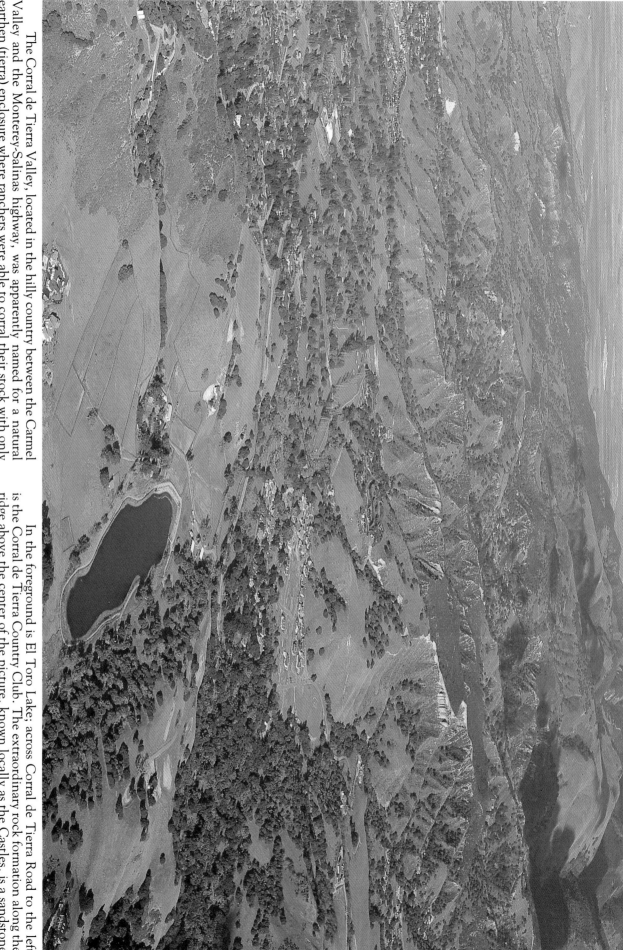

The Corral de Tierra Valley, located in the hilly country between the Carmel Valley and the Monterey-Salinas highway, was apparently named for a natural earthen (tierra) enclosure where ranchers were able to corral their stock with only a short fence on the side where a creek ran out. It was originally an idyllic vale of huge live oaks and Biblical green pastures, the setting for John Steinbeck's "The Pastures of Heaven."

In the foreground is El Toro Lake; across Corral de Tierra Road to the left is the Corral de Tierra Country Club. The extraordinary rock formation along the ridge above the center of the picture, known locally as the Castles, is a sandstone wall that has eroded into castellated badlands. You can see Mount Toro and Toro Regional Park at the upper right and the farm fields of the Salinas Valley at the upper left.

MONTEREY AND PACIFIC GROVE

Beyond Carmel Bay the Monterey Peninsula juts seaward. In the foreground is Corona Ridge.

Monterey in 1924 was still a quiet town surrounded by oak woodlands and a pine forest, recalling fondly its historic past as California's capital. The open space in the upper center is the Presidio of Monterey, with the harbor and Fisherman's Wharf to the upper right.

(*Opposite*) Seventy years later the town had become a booming city, thriving on tourism and recreation. Behind the marina at the lower left is the Custom House Plaza, part of Monterey State Historic Park. The Custom House itself, to the right of the plaza, is the oldest public building on the Pacific Coast, dating from the 1820s. To the right of the Custom House is Fisherman's Wharf. The green area at the center is the Presidio, entirely occupied now by the Defense Language Institute, which trains 4000 students from all military services in foreign languages. It was near the bluff at the foot of the Presidio that Vizcaíno landed in 1602 and Serra raised a cross in 1770.

The palatial Victorian Hotel Del Monte, shown here shortly before it burned to the ground in 1924, was built in 1887 (on the site of a smaller hotel that had also burned) by the owners of the Southern Pacific Railroad. "Hotel Del Monte" literally means "hotel of the grove," presumably referring to the pine and oak woodland roundabout.

(Opposite) In place of the burned Victorian palace rose a new hotel in 1926, this time appropriately in Spanish or early California style, in keeping with Monterey's traditions. It was designed under the guidance of S.F.B. Morse, grandnephew of the inventor of the telegraph. During World War II, the entire complex was taken over by the U.S. Navy and now is the U.S. Naval Postgraduate School, known (somewhat inaccurately) as the "Annapolis of the West." The freeway is State Highway 1. Upper right is the city of Seaside. Sand City straddles the freeway at the upper left.

This 1924 view shows an army encampment next to the S.F.B. Morse Racetrack, now the site of the Navy golf course (*opposite*). This was the site of the original Monterey airport. To the right of the golf course are the Monterey County Fairgrounds, where the Monterey Jazz Festival and other events take place. In the distance on the right are the red roofs of the Naval Postgraduate School and the lake on its campus.

The city of Pacific Grove is pleasantly bisected by its Municipal Golf Course, opened in 1932, Egan and Neville, architects. The city itself began as a Methodist retreat in 1875.

(*Opposite*) Spring-blossoming ice plant (*mesembryanthemum*) sends lavender fire along the bluff tops at Pacific Grove. Otter Point (lower right) is a good place to watch playful sea otters frolic offshore.

53

Stanford University's Hopkins Marine Station has carried on oceanic research in Pacific Grove since 1892, first on Lovers' Point, then since 1916 here on Point Cabrillo. It was the first marine laboratory on the Pacific Coast and was named for Timothy Hopkins, benefactor and adopted son of Mrs. Mark Hopkins.

(Opposite) The emerald waters in the lee of Lovers' Point in Pacific Grove offer excellent opportunities for still-water swimming and scuba diving in the offshore kelp beds, as the rafts indicate. Lovers' Point Park is the site of Gordon Neville's sculpture, "The Monarch Butterfly," honoring the insects that winter in the local groves. They provide the city with its nickname, "Butterfly Town, USA." The name of this promontory in some versions was originally "Lovers of Jesus Point," resulting from outdoor services held there during the town's history as a Methodist retreat. However, the story is dubious, and the present name seems amply justified by current activities.

Philanthropist David Packard, co-founder of the Hewlett-Packard Company, converted an old fish-processing plant at the north end of Cannery Row into the Monterey Bay Aquarium. There is a story that the idea for the structure was born when his two daughters, both marine biologists, asked their father for an aquarium for Christmas. He readily assented, thinking of a home-style fish tank. He found that he had agreed to a huge structure for the public display of the marine life of Monterey Bay. Before the building opened in 1984 he had spent $40 million on it, through the David and Lucille Packard Foundation. It turned out to be a good investment, however. Nearly two million paying visitors pass through the aquarium annually, viewing colossal glass tanks duplicating the bottom of Monterey Bay, with kelp forests and dozens of species of marine creatures from sharks to octopi. The research branch of the aquarium is the Monterey Bay Aquarium Research Institute, which operates out of Moss Landing (see page 65) with its ROV (remotely operated vehicle), probing the depths of the abyssal Monterey Canyon offshore, a near clone of the Grand Canyon of the Colorado.

59

Half encircled by the waters of El Estero are two cemeteries and above them the green playing field of Dennis the Menace Park, designed for children by Dennis's "father," cartoonist Hank Ketchum, a long-time local resident.

(*Opposite*) Along the northeast shore of the Monterey Peninsula are the Hopkins Marine Station, the Monterey Bay Aquarium, Cannery Row (where the old fish canneries described by John Steinbeck have been converted into shops and restaurants), and Monterey Harbor. Beyond, the bay shore curves past the white buildings of the Naval Postgraduate School. The first ridge in the background is Jacks Peak, and on the horizon are the peaks of the Ventana Wilderness.

In the rolling valley east of Monterey, the tortuous Laguna Seca ("dry lagoon") international raceway features motorcycle contests and sports-car races. It is part of a 542-acre county park with campsites, an off-road-vehicle area, and an amphitheater for music festivals and other events such as the visit of Pope John Paul II, attracting huge crowds. At the upper left is the Salinas Valley.

In the eastern extension of the city is the Monterey Peninsula Airport, with the Navy's golf course in the foreground. At the lower left are the Monterey County Fairgrounds. To the upper left of the airport is the community of Del Rey Oaks.

62

During World War II Fort Ord, on Highway 1 north of Monterey, became one of the nation's major military posts, training thousands of recruits for army combat duty. The entire reservation covers 44 square miles, an area about the size of San Francisco. Pictured here are the coastal areas of the fort, including housing for 15,000 soldiers and their families, and two 18-hole golf courses, the Black Horse Course and the Bayonet Course, named for the Bayonet (7th Infantry) Division that trained here in World War II. The Bayonet Course was designed in the 1950s

by the commanding general at Fort Ord, Bob McClellan, a championship amateur golfer. The Black Horse dates from the 1960s. Both are open to the public. In 1994 Fort Ord was one of the army bases closed under the Defense Department's "downsizing" process. Proposed for the site in the future are a 25,000-student campus of California State University, a University of California at Santa Cruz environmental research center, a public airport, an 8000-acre natural resources area, and a state park on the beachfront.

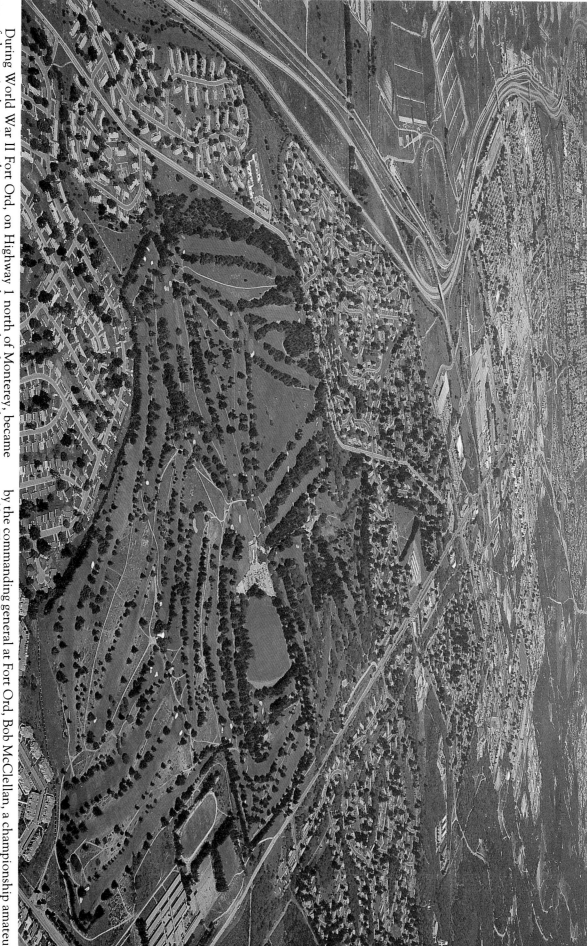

THE MONTEREY BAY COAST

Along the middle shoreline of Monterey Bay, agriculture creates abstract patterns in striking contrast to the rhythmic lines of the surf. The principal crops are artichokes and brussels sprouts, which benefit from the cool, foggy summers, and cut flowers, some of them grown in greenhouses.

Highway 1 cuts a broad swath through the artichoke fields near the mouth of the Salinas River. Most of this land has been reclaimed from the dunes, whose remnants are visible on the upper left. On the right is a shipping station for trucks loading vegetables from the region, including lettuce from the Salinas Valley.

(Opposite) Fifteen miles north of Monterey is Moss Landing, where various human and natural phenomena converge in intriguing combinations. Geologically this is the low point of the Monterey Bay coastline, evidently a result of a sinking or downwarping of the crust of the Earth here. One consequence is the existence of sloughs or estuaries where the sea has invaded the lowlands. On the far left is part of biologically rich Elkhorn Slough, a federal Estuarine Sanctuary. Just offshore is the head of the deep Monterey Canyon, which extends many miles to sea. It is studied at the Moss Landing Marine Station, operated by a group of California colleges. The largest of the industrial plants located here to take advantage of the waterways are a Pacific Gas & Electric power plant (left), billed as the second-largest non-nuclear plant in the world, and Kaiser Refractories.

(*Opposite*) At the north end of Monterey Bay is the city of Santa Cruz, where the San Lorenzo River, flowing down from the redwood canyons of the Santa Cruz Range, curves through urban land on its way to the bay. On the beachfront is the Santa Cruz Boardwalk, the last of California's traditional beach amusement zones.

Santa Cruz faces south, and its popular beaches are sheltered from the northwest winds that prevail along the rest of the coast. In this view from the west, the San Lorenzo River mouth and the boardwalk are above the center, just beyond the Municipal Pier. The green park on the right is at Santa Cruz Point, sometimes called Lighthouse Point. On the far side of the headland is Steamer Lane, which offers some of the best board surfing on the Pacific Coast and is the site of surfing tournaments.

One of the world's most spectacular college campuses is the University of California at Santa Cruz, spreading across ancient sea-carved terraces above the bay and extending into the redwood forests of the Santa Cruz Mountains. The campus plan was designed by its founder and first chancellor, Dean E. McHenry, to preserve pastures, historic farm buildings and open space and to include several separate colleges on the pattern of Oxford and Cambridge.

If you live here, you can almost pick out your home. From 67,000 feet up, this ultra-sharp NASA satellite photo (which changes green areas to red) reveals the contours of the Monterey Peninsula and adjacent areas. Monterey Harbor is at the curve of the shoreline at the upper center. To the left, Pacific Grove occupies the area stretching toward Point Pinos; the red streaks of its golf course are readily visible, as are the Pebble Beach fairways occupying much of the rest of the peninsula. In the center of the peninsula is Forest Lake, Pebble Beach's reservoir. The stretch of white sand is Carmel Beach. Carmel Valley and its golf courses are at the right, with Point Lobos State Reserve below.

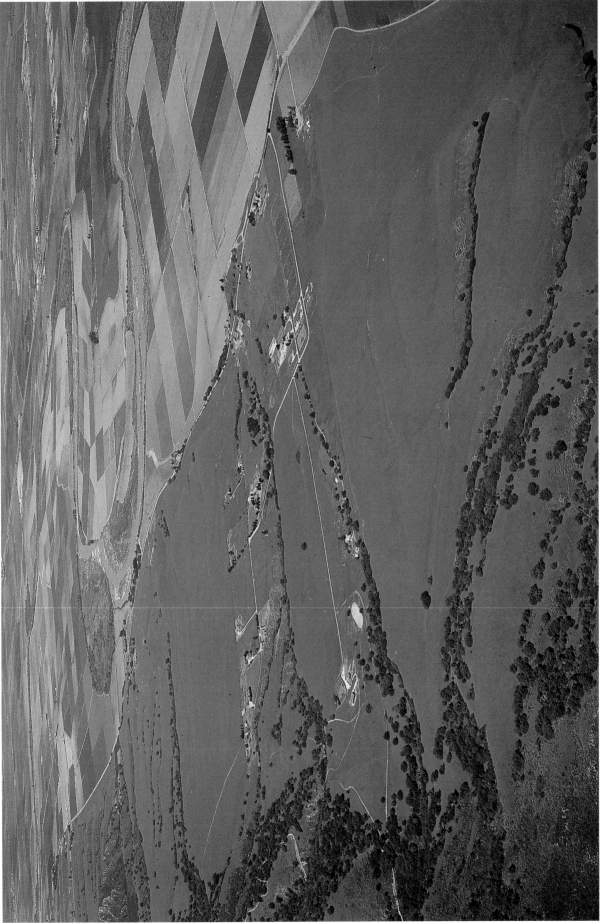

The rich farm fields of the Salinas Valley were the setting for stories by John Steinbeck, a native of Salinas. He wrote about this region in "The Long Valley," and used it again as his setting in "East of Eden." Agricultural and urban overdrafts of the Salinas Valley aquifer (the natural underground reservoir) fed by the Salinas River have lowered the water table and permitted salt water from Monterey Bay to advance underground, entering some of the wells.

(*Opposite*) The city of Salinas, seat of Monterey County, sprawls over agricultural fields, bisected by U.S. 101. In this view, looking southeast, the Northridge Shopping Center appears at the lower left. In the center of the picture are the California Rodeo Grounds, home of the annual Salinas Rodeo.

72

South of the city of Salinas, the Salinas River (flowing toward the lower left) meanders along the broad flat plain of the Salinas Valley amid fields of lettuce, strawberries, alfalfa, and other field crops. The valley, warmed by the summer sun but cooled by breezes from Monterey Bay, has earned the title, "Saladbowl of the World." The river is shown here at high water in winter, but in summer the river sinks into the sand, still flowing, and is responsible for another Salinas superlative, "the largest underground river in the world." On the right is the Santa Lucia Range; its seaward side is the Big Sur coast.

BIG SUR

Here we're back at the coast about a mile south of Carmel. The Carmelite Monastery, at the mouth of San Jose Creek, houses nuns of the Carmelite Order — the order of the three friars who accompanied the Vizcaíno expedition of 1603 and for whom Vizcaíno named "El Rio Carmelo." Monastery Beach, part of Carmel River State Beach, is popular with wet-suit divers, partly owing to its location at the head of the deep Carmel Canyon offshore. Because of the frequently heavy surf, the drownings that have occurred here have been responsible for the nickname "Mortuary Beach."

73

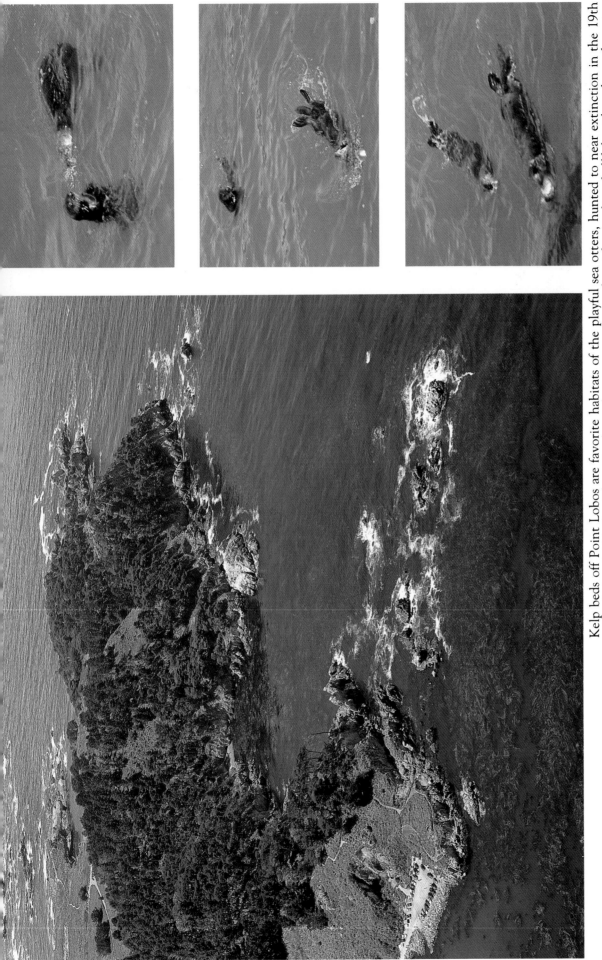

Kelp beds off Point Lobos are favorite habitats of the playful sea otters, hunted to near extinction in the 19th century for their valuable fur. The animals can be seen romping in the surf, pounding shellfish with rocks, and nursing and playing with their young. The waters are the nation's first marine reserve, created in 1960.

The high point of the ridge is Whalers' Knoll, supposedly Stevenson's model for Spyglass Hill on Treasure Island. Beyond the parking area and the treeless point at the upper left are Sea Lion Rocks, where the big mammals haul out to sleep and sometimes set up a great clamor of barking and roaring. Before it became a state park in 1933, the entire headland was planned for a residential subdivision.

(Opposite) Point Lobos State Reserve has been called "the greatest meeting of land and sea in the world." This point and Cypress Point in Pebble Beach (see page 6) are the only natural habitat of the Monterey cypress. It clings to the clifftop areas of fog and salt spray where other trees cannot survive and is sculpted into grotesque shapes by the sea wind. When Robert Louis Stevenson lived in Monterey, he frequently walked to the point, and it is believed to have been the model for his setting for "Treasure Island."

76

South of Point Lobos is the Carmel Highlands area. The cluster of buildings on the hillside is the Highlands Inn, centered around the original resort hotel built in 1917 by Frank Devendorf, founder of Carmel.

(*Opposite*) The Carmel Highlands area with its palatial homes extends southward past Wildcat Canyon (left) to Yankee Point (overleaf).

80

Beyond Yankee Point the Highlands ends at Malpaso Creek. The word means "bad pass," so named by Spanish explorers who found the steep canyon difficult to cross on their way along the coast. "Mal Paso Bridge" is the title of a poem by Robinson Jeffers (whose spelling differed from that of the map makers).

(Opposite) A mile or so south of Yankee Point civilization is left behind, and the Big Sur coast begins in earnest as Highway 1 traverses the wild clifftops above the roaring surf at the foot of the Santa Lucia Range. In the foreground is Soberanes Point (named for a pioneer family). Garrapata State Park begins here and extends south along the straight stretch of road to Garrapata Beach. The rock "island" of Point Sur with its lighthouse appears at the upper right; beyond it is Cooper Point at the mouth of the Big Sur River.

South of Bixby Creek, the highway traverses a portion of an ancient sea terrace. To the right the road is built in an obvious slide area and must be frequently repaired. Owing to its exposure to the northwest winds, this is known as Hurricane Point.

(*Opposite*) One of the great engineering challenges in the history of road building was the construction of State Highway 1 down the Big Sur Coast in the mid 1930s. This bridge over Bixby Creek is the largest of the bridges and the most-photographed symbol of Big Sur. The house on the point is on the site of Bixby Landing, where a cable extended from the point to ships loading timber and tanbark for San Francisco. In 1966 in a ceremony at Bixby Creek Bridge Lady Bird Johnson and Governor Edmund G. Brown dedicated the Big Sur route as the nation's first scenic highway.

Redwoods and associated vegetation grow in moist areas along canyon bottoms and on the northerly (mesic or moist) slopes of the ridges. The southerly (xeric or dry) slopes, more exposed to the sun, are too arid to support the forests. The greener areas along the ridgetops have been cleared of chaparral to provide grasses for grazing cattle. This is Garrapata Ridge, with Garrapata Canyon on the right, Palo Colorado (redwood) Canyon on the left.

(Opposite) One of the highest points visible from the highway is Pico Blanco (white peak), so called because of its limestone summit, which has been the objective of a mining company that would like to quarry the valuable rock. A small test quarry already exists on the far side; trucks hauling the limestone used the road visible here. Controversy swirls around the mountain like a summer fog as environmentalists and miners engage in political combat. Virgin redwoods grow in the canyon of Little Sur River to the left. On the horizon are the even higher summits of the Ventana Wilderness.

Like Mont-Saint-Michel off the coast of France, Point Sur is an island that has been connected to the mainland. Sheltering the coast here like a breakwater, the island has enabled the waves to deposit sand on its lee side, creating a peninsula that is sometimes overridden by large storm waves. The lighthouse at the left end of the rock was completed in 1889, and its powerful beam and fog horn still warn ships to steer clear of the dangerous coast.

(*Opposite*) Off this coast in spring, summer and early fall, persistent northwest winds from the ocean push the surface waters offshore, causing an upwelling of frigid water from the sunless depths. The cold water acts as a refrigerant and chills the air above it, causing the invisible water vapor in the air to condense into the great fog bank that intermittently hangs along this coast, invades the mouths of coastal canyons like an aerial flood, and provides moisture for the redwoods during the rainless summers. Redwoods grow on the California coast only in the areas reached by the summer fogs, which often penetrate farther inland than they do here. The road cut is the old coast road from the era before Highway 1 was built.

Almost hidden in the oaks on this point is Nepenthe, a prime Big Sur gathering spot for residents and visitors alike and one of the few restaurants along this coast. The three-syllabled name comes from a mythical Egyptian drug supposed to bring surcease from sorrow. The serene atmosphere and the superb views of mountains and ocean are likely to do that. The redwood cabin next to the restaurant was built in 1925 for Big Sur hikers, and the property was bought in 1944 by Orson Welles as a retreat for himself and his new wife, Rita Hayworth. Neither the retreat nor the marriage lasted long. Three years later Welles sold the land to Bill and

Lolly Fassett, who enlisted architect Rowan Maiden, a colleague of Frank Lloyd Wright, to design a building that would harmonize with its natural surroundings. Since its opening in 1949, it has been operated by two generations of the Fassett family.

The yellow plant on the hillsides above the road is French broom, a non-native that aggressively takes over from the native vegetation to the despair of botanists but nevertheless supplies a swath of spring color to the hillsides.

In 1983, "El Niño" storms deluged California with rain, sent giant waves to batter the cliffs, and washed out or undermined several stretches of the Big Sur highway, which was closed to through traffic for more than a year.

On a narrow section of an ancient terrace above the ocean is the Esalen Institute, named for the native inhabitants of the region. It has sponsored seminars, symposiums, and classes on New Age human-potential subjects since the 1960s. At the lower far right is the structure housing the hot springs, which have attracted bathers beginning with the Indians. Here you can luxuriate in the warm waters as you gaze at the ocean and listen to the sounds of the surf and perhaps the barking of sea lions.

(*Opposite*) Eastward into the Santa Lucias from the coast is the vast Ventana Wilderness, a unit of Los Padres National Forest. "Ventana" is Spanish for "window," and the area was named for a window-like opening near Ventana Peak. Most of the rugged terrain is accessible only to equally rugged hikers over trails that switchback up and down steep ridges but provide an unforgettable experience of wooded canyons, rivers, streams, and upland meadows, with such intriguing names as Buckskin Flat, Sulphur Springs, Hanging Valley, Lost Valley, and Last Chance.

92

Flat terraces like this one were carved by the Pacific when the Santa Lucia Range paused in its sporadic rise from the ocean long enough for waves to plane off this shelf. As the range rose again, it lifted the terrace high above sea level; along the greater part of the coast the terrace has been eroded away, undermined by the kind of waves that created it.

(*Opposite*) Another broad terrace appears at San Simeon Point, at the south end of the Big Sur coast. The point provided a natural harbor for mining tycoon George Hearst to develop a ranch here in the 1860s. His son, William Randolph Hearst, used the harbor in the 1920s to ship in materials for the "castle" he built on a commanding hilltop of the 240,000-acre ranch. Ranch buildings and the hamlet of San Simeon are in the center of the picture, and the castle is on the summit of "Camp Hill," where George Hearst used to camp with his family and friends.

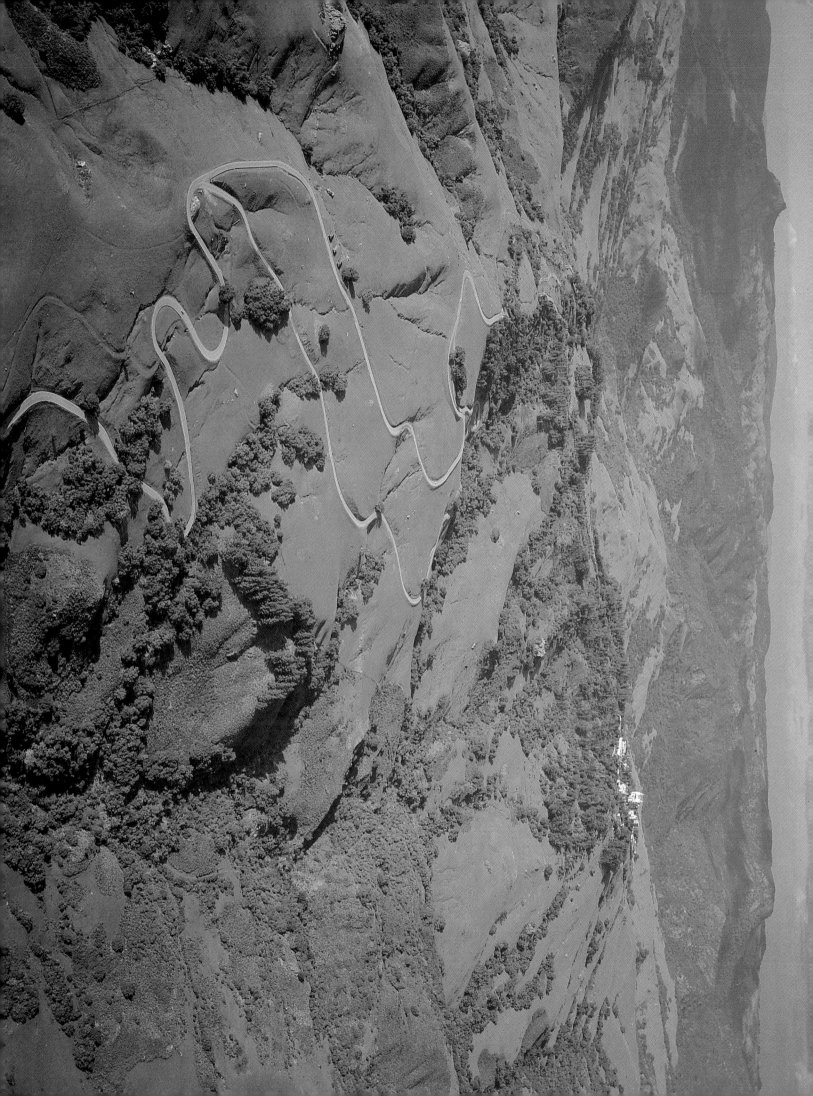

On what he called "La Cuesta Encantada" — the enchanted crest — Hearst, working with architect Julia Morgan, built this Spanish Renaissance complex: "La Casa Grande," guest houses, and pools, a lavishly appointed spread that would have dazzled a Roman emperor. Here he housed his incredible collection of art and antiques and entertained world celebrities for three decades.

(*Opposite*) After the death of William Randolph Hearst the ranch was donated to the state by his heirs and has been a California state park since 1958. Visitors (with reservations) park at the bottom of the hill and ride a shuttle bus along the road to the fantasy on the summit.

OTHER BOOKS BY ROBERT CAMERON: *Hardcover, one hundred sixty full color pages, 11 x 14 inches.*

ABOVE SEATTLE with Emmett Watson
ABOVE CHICAGO with Tim Samuelson and Cheryl Kent
ABOVE SAN FRANCISCO with Herb Caen
ABOVE LOS ANGELES with Jack Smith
ABOVE SAN DIEGO with Neil Morgan
ABOVE YOSEMITE with Harold Gilliam
ABOVE LONDON with Alistair Cooke
ABOVE PARIS with Pierre Salinger
ABOVE HAWAII
ABOVE WASHINGTON (D.C.)
ABOVE NEW YORK with George Plimpton and Paul Goldberger

Softcover, ninety-six full color pages, 9 x 12 inches.

ABOVE MACKINAC with Phil Porter

Available from Cameron and Company and at fine Booksellers.